Comptroller of the Currency
Administrator of National Banks

Lease Financing

Comptroller's Handbook

January 1998

A

Assets

Lease Financing

Table of Contents

Introduction 1
   Background 1
   Statutory and Regulatory Authority for Leasing 2
      Subpart A) General Provisions 3
      Subpart B) CEBA Leases 4
      Subpart C) Leases under 12 USC 24 (Seventh) 4
      12 CFR 7.1000(d) 5
      Limits on National Bank Leasing Activities 5
   Examining Leasing Operations 6
   Risks Associated with Lease Financing 6
   Categories of Leases 10
   Accounting for Leases 12
      Investment Tax Credit 14
   Documenting a Lease 15
   Property Acquired for Future Leasing Activities 15
   Lending Limits 15

Examination Procedures 17
   General Procedures 17
   Quantity of Risk 19
      All Leases 19
      Delinquent and Defaulted Leases 21
      Direct Financing and Operating Leases 22
      Leveraged Leases 24
      Commitments to Lease 27
      Off-Lease Property 27
      Property Acquired for Future Leasing Activity 27
      Compliance with Laws, Rules, and Regulations 28
   Quality of Risk Management 30
      Policy 30
      Processes 30
      Personnel 32
      Controls 33
   Conclusion Procedures 36

Appendix 38
   Examples 38

Glossary 46

References 49

Background

A lease is an agreement allowing one party to use another's property, plant, or equipment for a stated period of time in exchange for consideration. Leases have become more prevalent as businesses and consumers look for alternatives to finance the acquisition of fixed assets. A lease agreement involves at least two parties) a lessor (such as a bank), who owns the property, and a lessee, who uses the property. The lessor, essentially a creditor in the transaction, is repaid from a combination of lease or rental payments, tax benefits, and proceeds from the sale or re-lease of the property at the end of the lease term.

Although leasing is often thought of as a modern day financing technique, indications are that leasing transactions took place around 2000 B.C., when Sumerian farmers leased tools from temple priests. The basics of leasing have changed little since that time. Over the years, the strength of the leasing industry has been its resiliency and its ability to make the most of the changing business environment.

Leasing is the most widely used method of personal property financing in the United States today. For bank lessors, leasing is another competitive product that can satisfy the needs of bank customers; leases may be safer than other bank products because the transactions are secured; and leases are generally more profitable than commercial loans because of advantages inherent in their structure, such as tax benefits.

Leasing is a way for lessees (customers) to conserve capital because, in effect, they obtain 100 percent financing. Depending on the structure of the lease, the risks of ownership (such as the possibility that the product will become obsolete) can be transferred to the lessor. Tax benefits could also be transferred to a lessor, resulting in lower lease payments to the lessee. Operating leases are off-balance-sheet, which may improve certain of the lessee's key financial ratios.

A special type of transaction, the sale-leaseback, allows the owner of a piece of property (usually real estate) to raise funds while retaining use of the property. In such a transaction (actually two separate transactions), the owner of the property sells the property and immediately leases it back. There is no physical transfer of the property. From a safety and soundness perspective, leases that result from sale-leaseback transactions should be reviewed in essentially the same manner as other leases.

National banks may engage in leases for agricultural, business, commercial, or consumer purposes. As a general rule, they may acquire property to be leased only after the bank enters into a legally binding commitment to lease or a legally binding written agreement indemnifying the bank against loss in connection with the acquisition of the leased property.

National banks may act as lessors and finance "net leases" for personal property. In a net lease, the bank is not directly or indirectly obligated to assume the expenses of maintaining the property. This does not prohibit the bank from arranging for an independent third party to provide servicing, repair, or maintenance of the leased property during the lease term.

A national bank is prohibited from being a general partner in a commercial endeavor. Therefore, when a national bank sells participations in a lease, it must avoid becoming a general partner, generally by entering into a trust arrangement or forming a limited partnership.

A consumer lease is defined by the Consumer Leasing Act of 1976, as amended (15 USC 1667). The law is implemented by the Federal Reserve Board's Regulation M (12 CFR Part 213). This handbook section is not a guide to compliance with applicable consumer protection laws and regulations; to obtain such guidance, consult the "Other Consumer Protection Laws and Regulations" booklet of the Comptroller's Handbook.

A glossary of leasing terms follows this booklet's appendix and precedes its references page.

Statutory and Regulatory Authority for Leasing

Since 1977, banks have been allowed to provide personal property leases that are the functional equivalent of loans. Such activity is permitted under 12 USC 24 (Seventh) as being incidental to the business of banking. The Comptroller's interpretation permitting national banks to execute leases was upheld in a court decision arising from the case of M&M Leasing Corp. v. Seattle First National Bank. In that case, the court held that leasing is permissible provided the lease is the functional equivalent of a loan. Following that decision, the OCC issued an interpretive ruling (former IR 7.3400, effective June 12, 1979) that gave national banks the authority to enter into net leases that are the functional equivalent of loans. A lease under this section must be a full-payout lease. In addition, any unguaranteed portion of the estimated residual value of the leased property the bank relies upon to yield a full return must not exceed 25 percent of the original cost of the property to the bank. There is no regulatory limit on the aggregate amount of such leases a bank can carry on its books.

The Competitive Equality Banking Act of 1987 (CEBA) was the first statute to specifically allow national banks to engage in leasing. Section 108 of CEBA amended 12 USC 24 by adding a 10th part that specifically allows a bank to invest in tangible personal property for lease financing transactions on a net lease basis. A lease under this section, like a Section 24 (Seventh) lease, must be a full-payout lease. There is no limit on the amount of estimated residual value the bank may rely upon to satisfy the full-payout requirement. Investment in leases under this part, however, cannot exceed 10 percent of a national bank's consolidated total assets. National banks should maintain documentation identifying these CEBA leases.

Effective in 1991, the OCC issued 12 CFR 23, which allows lease financing of personal property by national banks under 12 USC 24 (Seventh) and 12 USC 24 (10th). The OCC revised the regulation effective January 17, 1997. 12 CFR 23 contains three subparts:

- Subpart A applies to all lease financing transactions,

- Subpart B addresses additional requirements applicable to CEBA leases, and

- Subpart C addresses a bank's authority to enter into net leases that are the functional equivalent of loans.

Subpart A) General Provisions

All lease financing transactions in national banks must follow the general provisions contained in Subpart A (12 CFR 23.1 through 23.6). Under these provisions, the lease must be a "full-payout lease" on a "net lease" basis. A full-payout lease is one where the bank reasonably expects to realize its full investment in the leased property (and financing costs) from rentals, estimated tax benefits, and the estimated residual value of the property at the expiration of the lease term. A net lease is one that does not, directly or indirectly, obligate the bank to provide maintenance, insurance, parts, or accessories for the asset. (Note: national banks are not prohibited from arranging for an independent third-party provider to perform these services at the expense of the lessee).

As a general rule, a national bank can acquire specific property to be leased only after it has entered into a conforming lease, obtained a legally binding agreement indemnifying the bank against loss in connection with the acquisition, or entered into a legally binding commitment to lease. There is one exception to the general rule. A national bank may acquire property to be leased if the acquisition is consistent with the bank's current leasing business or with a business plan to expand the bank's existing leasing business or to enter the leasing business. The bank's aggregate investment in property held pursuant to this exception can not exceed 15 percent of the bank's capital and surplus.

Upon the expiration of the lease (or the default of the lessee), the bank must dispose of or re-lease the property as soon as practicable. Generally, national banks must do so within five years of the date the bank acquires the legal right to possess or control the property. The OCC may extend the holding period for as many as five additional years if the bank can demonstrate that an additional holding period is clearly necessary.

This subpart also requires banks to maintain separate records for leases subject to 12 USC 24 (Seventh) and 12 USC 24 (10th) and subjects all leases to lending limits and restrictions on transactions with affiliates.

Subpart B) CEBA Leases

This subpart (12 CFR 23.10 through 23.12) governs the additional requirements for CEBA leases. Under 12 USC 24 (10th) national banks may, on a net lease basis, invest in tangible personal property, including vehicles, manufactured homes, machinery, equipment, furniture, or other types of tangible personal property. The aggregate book value of CEBA leases cannot exceed 10 percent of consolidated total bank assets. This subpart also establishes a minimum lease term of 90 days.

Subpart C) Leases under 12 USC 24 (Seventh)

This subpart (12 CFR 23.20 through 23.22) governs leases entered into under 12 USC 24 (Seventh) and incorporates, with changes, the provisions previously contained in an interpretative ruling. Under this subpart, a national bank may be the lessor of personal property on net leases that are the functional equivalent of loans. The bank's recovery of its investment plus financing costs must depend upon the creditworthiness of the lessee and any guarantor of the residual value. The unguaranteed portion of the estimated residual value relied upon by the bank to yield a full return must not exceed 25 percent of the property cost. However, calculations of estimated residual values for leases with governmental entities may be based upon reasonable expectation that transactions will be renewed.

12 CFR 7.1000(d)

This interpretive ruling allows national banks to enter into leases for public facilities with municipalities or other public authorities. A national bank may purchase or construct a municipal building, e.g., a school or other similar public facility, and, as holder of legal title, may lease the facility to a municipality or other public authority. The only limit is that the municipality or authority must have sufficient resources to pay all rentals as they become due. Leases under this interpretation must provide that, upon expiration of the lease, the lessee will become the owner of the building or facility.

Limits on National Bank Leasing Activities

Leases entered into by the bank are subject to the following limits:

- The 12 USC 371c and 371c-1 limits on transactions with affiliates.

- The 12 USC 84 lending limits.

- Limits in 12 USC 24 (Seventh) or (10th).

- The relevant limits in 12 CFR 23.

Calculations under these rules may differ from those specified by the Financial Accounting Standards Board. For example, the outstanding obligation of the lessee under 12 USC 84 is the sum of the present value of both the lease payments and the residual value of the property, rather than the calculation under Statement of Financial Accounting Standard (SFAS) 13 (see "Accounting" in this booklet for more information).

The outstanding obligation of the lessee under a leveraged lease is calculated in much the same way (see "Categories of Leases" in this booklet for more information on leveraged leases). In a leveraged lease, however, the unamortized balance of the nonrecourse debt is deducted from the present value elements. This deduction recognizes that nonrecourse debt is not an obligation of the lessee to the bank lessor.

Similarly, when calculating the total volume of CEBA leases to apply the 12 USC 24 (10th) limit of 10 percent, one subtracts the nonrecourse debt the bank has incurred to finance the acquisition of the leased property (see 12 CFR 23.10). This treatment more accurately reflects the bank's exposure and is consistent with the lending limit treatment.

Examining Leasing Operations

An examiner should be sure that a leasing department performs in a safe and sound manner. Management should have a system that identifies, measures, monitors, and controls the bank's risk exposure. To determine whether the system is effective, the examiner must understand the statutory and regulatory background of leasing, the reasons banks become involved in leasing, the risks involved, the different types of leases, and how to account for leases.

For the most part, a leasing examination is very much like any other examination of asset quality. The examiner seeks to understand and evaluate the bank's credit policies or practices and portfolio administration. Guidelines on examining loan portfolios appear in other sections of the Comptroller's Handbook devoted to assets. "Loan Portfolio Management," in particular, should be helpful. This booklet deals primarily with matters unique to leasing.

Risks Associated with Lease Financing

For purposes of the OCC's discussion of risk, examiners assess banking risk relative to its impact on capital and earnings. From a supervisory perspective, risk is the potential that events, expected or unanticipated, may have an adverse impact on the bank's capital or earnings. The OCC has defined nine categories of risk for bank supervision purposes. These risks are credit, interest rate, liquidity, price, foreign exchange, transaction, compliance, strategic, and reputation. These categories are not mutually exclusive; any product or service may expose the bank to multiple risks. For analysis and discussion purposes, however, the OCC identifies and assesses the risks separately.

The applicable risks associated with lease financing are credit, interest rate, liquidity, transaction, and compliance. These risks are discussed more fully in the following paragraphs.

Credit Risk

Credit risk is the risk to earnings or capital arising from an obligor's failure to meet the terms of any contract with the bank or otherwise to perform as agreed. Credit risk is found in all activities where success depends on counterparty, issuer, or borrower performance. It arises any time bank funds are extended, committed, invested, or otherwise exposed through actual or implied contractual agreements, whether reflected on or off the balance sheet.

In assessing credit risk, the examiner must realize that the rental payments on a lease carry substantially the same risk as payments on a secured loan. Leases should be reviewed as if they were loans, using the same definitions to classify them, the same methods to allocate reserves, and the same characteristics to determine accrual status. Ownership of the underlying property is an additional consideration in evaluating a lease transaction. If the lessee defaults, the bank, as owner, usually can recover the property expeditiously.

Before entering into a lease, a national bank must reasonably expect to realize the return of its full investment in the leased property, and the estimated cost of financing the property over the lease term, from a combination of rental payments, estimated tax benefits, and estimated residual value of the property when the lease term expires. For each lease, the examiner should review the risks affecting collectibility from each of these three sources by ensuring that the bank has established the creditworthiness of the lessee, has considered potential changes in tax benefits, and has periodically assessed the value of the leased property.

Interest Rate Risk

Interest rate risk is the risk to earnings or capital arising from movements in interest rates. From an economic perspective, a bank focuses on the sensitivity of the value of its assets, liabilities and revenues to changes in interest rates. Interest rate risk arises from differences between the timing of rate changes and the timing of cash flows (repricing risk); from changing rate relationships among different yield curves affecting bank activities (basis risk); from changing rate relationships across the spectrum of maturities (yield curve risk); and from interest-related options embedded in bank products (options risk). The evaluation of interest rate risk must consider the impact of complex, illiquid hedging strategies or products, and also the potential impact on fee income that is sensitive to changes in interest rates. In those situations where trading is separately managed, this refers to structural positions and not trading portfolios.

Like loans, leases are subject to interest rate risk. Loans have an explicit interest rate, whereas a lease transaction is negotiated and underwritten based on an implicit interest rate. This implicit rate is derived from a fixed rate of interest for most leases in the banking industry. Typically, the interest rate risk to the bank is the same as if the bank were making a loan with an explicit fixed interest rate. Fixed interest rates expose the bank to interest rate risk when interest rates change (which they do because of competitive or economic forces). Prepayment or early termination of leases subjects the bank to additional interest rate interest. When the bank funds a lease, management should consider the potential impact on earnings arising from interest rate risk and, through asset-liability management, should attempt to mitigate the risks associated with fixed rate lease financing. Banks can use a variety of techniques to manage interest rate risk, such as adjusting the maturity and payment frequency of the lease, basing the implicit interest rate on a floating rate, and hedging the fixed rate exposure.

Liquidity Risk

Liquidity risk is the risk to earnings or capital arising from a bank's inability to meet its obligations when they come due, without incurring unacceptable losses. Liquidity risk includes the inability to manage unplanned decreases or changes in funding sources. Liquidity risk also arises from the bank's failure to recognize or address changes in market conditions that affect the ability to liquidate assets quickly and with minimal loss in value.

Examiners normally assess an asset's liquidity risk in terms of its expected life and the ease with which it can be converted into cash. A lease's liquidity risk is no different. Examiners must evaluate the terms of the leases and determine whether anything could affect the bank's expected yield on the leasing portfolio. To the extent that such factors are present, the examiner would assess any expected needs to liquidate portions of the portfolio to meet other funding requirements or take advantage of other opportunities. Concentrations by obligor, industry, or property type must be carefully reviewed to evaluate the liquidity risk.

Transaction Risk

Transaction risk is the risk to earnings or capital arising from problems with service or product delivery. This risk is a function of internal controls, information systems, employee integrity, and operating processes. Transaction risk exists in all products and services.

One important component of transaction risk that is unique to leasing is residual, or property, risk. Residual value is an estimate of future value — that is, an estimate of the amount that will be realized upon disposal or re-lease of the property at the end of the lease term. A bank that does not properly control residual risk may be unable to recover its investment.

One way of exerting such control is periodically to evaluate leased property for misuse, obsolescence, or market decline, any of which can rapidly depreciate the value of the property. Collateral may be valued by appraisal, engineering estimates, broker/dealers' prices for similar used assets, and past recoveries on similar assets. Examiners must carefully review how the property is valued initially and periodically throughout the lease to determine whether the residual value is reasonable. If a bank uses a model to derive residual values, the examiner must determine whether assumptions used in the model are reasonable. A bank can manipulate income by projecting unreasonably high residuals, and thereby expose itself to unwarranted risk during the lease term. Examiners should evaluate residuals on individual leases as part of the overall assessment of transaction risk in the bank's portfolio.

Lessors whose returns depend substantially on tax benefits risk losing them if the lessee defaults or tax laws change. Some lessor/owners may claim accelerated depreciation on the cost of the property, which can produce deferred tax benefits because of the difference between book and tax accounting. Some properties placed in service before January 1, 1986, offered an investment tax credit to lessors. In such circumstances, the bank should evaluate its present and anticipated future tax position and future money rates. If there is a default and leases depending on tax benefits are "unwound," the bank may be required to recapture tax benefits taken to date. That could significantly increase the bank's exposure to loss. Examiners should review the bank's exposure to changes in its tax position. When the exposure is caused by changes in tax laws, the examiner should determine whether the borrower indemnifies the lessor against that risk.

Transaction risk is also present when a bank leases to municipalities (state and local governments). The risk is specifically nonappropriation. Municipalities may cancel personal property leases if funds are not appropriated. In the course of reviewing leases with municipalities, examiners should determine the likelihood of nonappropriation, an assessment that should be based on the type of property leased. A provision in all municipal leases should prohibit the municipality from leasing or purchasing similar property if the lease is canceled. In general, the agreement should also include evidence of appropriation for the first fiscal period.

The policies, procedures, practices, systems, and controls that allow management and the board of directors to monitor the leasing department's operations should be similar to those used to monitor the loan department. Incorrect assumptions or changes in market conditions affecting the property could make it difficult for a bank to recover its investment. Managers require accurate and complete MIS information in order to monitor payment status, collections, lease run-offs, residual position, and concentrations within the leasing portfolio. Reviews by either the internal or external auditors can help the bank assess the effectiveness of its controls on transaction risk.

Compliance Risk

Compliance risk is the risk to earnings or capital arising from violations of, or nonconformance with, laws, rules, regulations, prescribed practices, or ethical standards. Compliance risk also arises in situations where the laws or rules governing certain bank products or activities of the bank's clients may be ambiguous or untested. Compliance risk exposes the institution to fines, civil money penalties, payment of damages, and the voiding of contracts. Compliance risk can lead to a diminished reputation, reduced franchise value, limited business opportunities, lessened expansion potential, and lack of contract enforceability.

Compliance risk in the form of litigation, settlements, or judgments affects leasing. If there are problems with documentation, the bank could lose its contractual rights under a lease. It could lose its ability to realize tax benefits or take advantage of the rights of property ownership, including repossession and sale. (See "Documenting a Lease" in this booklet for more information regarding lease documentation.)

Compliance risk affects leasing much as it does lending. Therefore, a bank's compliance procedures for leasing activities should be very similar to those for lending activities. The bank's compliance efforts should focus on 12 USC 24 (Seventh), 12 USC 24 (10th), 12 USC 84, 12 USC 371c and 371c-1, 12 CFR 23, 12 CFR 32, 12 CFR 7.1000(d), Regulation M and other consumer protection laws and regulations, and SFAS 13.

Categories of Leases

A lease must be correctly categorized before its proper accounting treatment can be established. To categorize a lease properly, one uses the facts and circumstances surrounding the origination of the transaction and whether or not substantially all of the benefits and risks of ownership are transferred to the lessee. (See "Accounting" in this booklet for more information.)

For accounting and reporting purposes, the lessee must identify each lease as one of two alternative types) capital or operating. A capital lease transfers substantially all the risks and benefits of ownership to the lessee. Any other kind of lease is an operating lease.

The lessor must categorize each lease into one of four types — sales-type, direct financing, leveraged, or operating.

A sales-type lease is one that is structured so that the lessor (generally a manufacturer or dealer of property) not only obtains interest income but also recognizes a profit or loss on the transaction. Such recognition can occur only if the value of the property is different from the cost when the lease expires. It may be useful to see this type of transaction as tantamount to a sale. A common sales-type lease is the agreement between an automobile dealership and a customer. In that circumstance, the lessor (dealership) is leasing the automobile in lieu of selling it. National bank lessors normally do not offer sales-type leases.

A direct financing lease is one in which the lessor's only source of revenue is interest. The lessor (generally a bank or other financial institution) buys an asset and leases it to the lessee. This transaction is an alternative to the more customary lending arrangement in which a borrower uses the loan proceeds to purchase an asset. A direct financing lease is the functional equivalent of a loan.

A leveraged lease is a specialized form of direct financing lease that involves at least three parties: a lessee, a long-term creditor (the debt participant), and a lessor (the equity participant). This type of lease transaction is complex because of its size, the number of parties involved, legal demands, and the unique advantages to all parties. Because of the legal expenses and administrative costs involved, leveraged leasing usually finances only large capital property projects. The structure of leveraged leases allows them to be tailored to best meet the tax needs of the parties involved.

In a leveraged lease, the lessor that purchases the property provides only a percentage (usually 20 to 40 percent) of the capital needed. After obtaining this substantial leverage in the transaction, the lessor takes out a nonrecourse loan for the balance of the purchase price from long-term lenders (the debt participants). That borrowing is secured by a first lien on the property, assignment of the lease, and assignment of the lease rental payments. The lessor, as the owner, is able to take accelerated depreciation and to claim any available investment tax credit based on the total cost of the property. The lessor also retains the residual value rights to the property at the end of the lease period. Under this arrangement, the lessee has use of the property at a lower cost in exchange for leaving the tax benefits with the lessor. This trade-off ideally produces an attractive rate of return for the lessor and financing for the lessee at a cost below the lessee's normal borrowing rate.

When the purchase price of the property is large, a leveraged lease may involve several lessors and debt participants. In such cases, an owner trustee generally holds title to the property and represents the lessors. Or an indenture trustee may hold the mortgage on the property on behalf of the debt participants.

Because of the complexity of leveraged leases, they should be offered only by banks with appropriate expertise. Examiners should determine whether the personnel who structure and administer leases are qualified in that area and have a working knowledge of applicable tax laws and regulations.

An operating lease does not transfer the risk and benefits of ownership to the lessee. The lessor, as owner of the property, retains legal title. In this transaction, the lessor is entitled to any tax benefits of ownership (such as accelerated depreciation). The lessor also retains the rights to the property's residual value at the end of the term. In most operating leases the term of the initial lease agreement is significantly shorter than the economic life of the property.

Accounting for Leases

As discussed under "Categories of Leases" in this booklet, a lease must be properly categorized to establish its proper accounting treatment. The first step in categorizing a lease is to determine whether or not the risks and benefits of ownership have been substantially transferred to the lessee.

According to the SFAS 13, "Accounting for Leases," substantially all of the risks and benefits of ownership are considered to be transferred to the lessee if, at inception, the lease meets at least one of the following criteria:

- The lease transfers ownership of the property to the lessee by the end of the lease term.

- The lease contains a bargain purchase option.

- The lease term equals at least 75 percent of the estimated economic life of the leased property. Economic life is defined as the period during which the property can be used economically by one or more users for the purpose that it was intended at the inception of the lease. Estimated economic life and estimated useful life (for depreciation purposes) are not necessarily the same. For example, a bank may use a shorter useful life and higher salvage value for depreciation purposes if its policy is to dispose of assets before the end of the assets' economic lives.

- The present value of the minimum lease payments at the beginning of the lease term equals at least 90 percent of the fair market value less any investment tax credit retained by the lessor. (Note: A lessor should compute the present value using the interest rate implicit in the lease. A lessee should compute the present value using the lessee's incremental borrowing rate unless the implicit rate is available and lower.)

For the lessee, any lease that meets any one of those criteria is accounted for as a capital lease. All other leases are accounted for as operating leases.

For the lessor, determining accounting treatment is somewhat more complicated. If the lease meets any one of the four criteria listed above and both of the criteria set forth below, the lease is further categorized as either a sales-type, direct financing, or leveraged lease depending upon the conditions present at the inception of the lease (see "Categories of Leases" in this booklet for a discussion of the different conditions defining those types):

- Collectibility of the minimum lease payments is reasonably predictable.

- The amount of unreimbursable costs yet to be incurred by the lessor under the lease is substantially predictable.

Leases that do not meet these criteria are accounted for as operating leases on the lessor's books. For direct financing leases, bank lessors should record the lease in an amount equal to the sum of the aggregate minimum lease payments (including any guaranteed residual value), the unguaranteed residual value, and any available investment tax credit. Any excess of those items over the actual cost of the property leased is recorded as a liability, unearned income. Lease payments made are applied to reduce the asset account. Unearned income is accrued over the life of the lease using the effective income method (a constant periodic rate of return). Initial direct costs also are amortized over the lease term. Banks may use other methods of recognizing income if the results are not materially different.

When accounting for leveraged leases, the lessor's net investment (gross investment less unearned income and deferred taxes) is recorded as it would be in a direct financing lease, but principal and interest on the nonrecourse debt is netted out. Based on an analysis of projected cash flow for the lease term, unearned and deferred income is recognized as income at a constant rate only when the net investment is positive. In years when the net investment is zero or negative, no income is to be recognized. As a result of the timing of the tax benefits, the lessor's net investment declines during the early years of the lease and rises in the later years.

Bank lessors account for operating leases by recording the cost of the property leased as an "other asset." That asset, less the residual value at the end of the lease, is depreciated over the estimated economic life of the property, following the bank's normal depreciation policy or practice. Lease rental payments are taken directly into income over the life of the lease as they become due and receivable (accrual accounting). Any initial direct costs generally are amortized over the lease term as revenue is recognized. If such costs are immaterial, they may be expensed as incurred.

According to SFAS 13, the lessor is required to review the residual position of all leases at least once each year. If there is a permanent decline in the property's value, the estimate of residual value must be revised. The loss that arises in the net investment is to be recognized in the period of the decline, through a charge to operations. Write-downs resulting from revised estimates of residual value should not be recorded by adding to the allowance for loan and lease losses or reserve accounts. If the decline in the property's value is temporary, no charge at all is required. Estimated residual values must never be revised upward. Banks should never make provisions to the allowance for loan and lease losses or reserve accounts for potential declines in residual values. (A "potential decline" is one that is not tied to an acknowledged decline in the property's value.)

Lease renewals and extensions are accounted for differently depending on the type of renewal or extension. Any adjustments must be reflected in the current period's income.

When a lease is terminated, the lessor should remove any remaining net investment from the books and record the leased property as an asset at the lower of cost, present fair value, or current carrying value. Adjustments should be reflected in the current period's operating results. If the leased property is sold at the end of the lease, the gain or loss is calculated by comparing the net proceeds from the sale to the residual value account balance. Again, any gain or loss should be reflected in income during the current period. The maximum holding period for off-lease property is five years, unless the OCC specifically approves a longer one. Upon expiration of the holding period, any balances in the leasing accounts related to that property must be completely written off.

The appendix contains examples demonstrating a lessor's accounting treatment of an operating lease, a direct financing lease, and a leveraged lease.

Investment Tax Credit

Investment tax credits are available only for property placed in service before 1985, except for transition property. The credit was repealed effective January 1, 1986, and the Internal Revenue Code was amended. Transition properties are assets for which certain actions were taken before 1986 or for which a binding written contract existed before that year and which were placed in service within specified time periods.

Documenting a Lease

When a bank is asked to purchase property for lease, it may issue a commitment to lease describing the property, the cost, and the lease terms. After these terms are reached in negotiations between the bank and its customer, an order is usually written asking the bank to purchase the property. After purchasing the property, the bank arranges for any necessary delivery and installation.

The bank should have a legally binding agreement to lease and a lease contract that incorporates all the points in the commitment letter. The lease contract also should outline the rights of all parties in the event of default. The lease contract is usually signed at the same time as the order to purchase and the agreement to lease. Each lease is an individual contract written to fulfill the lessee's needs; consequently, there are many variations in lease terms and conditions. Every lease should convey a clear understanding of the lessee's positive right to use the property for a specific period of time, and every lease should make the payment plans irrevocable.

Property Acquired for Future Leasing Activities

Banks can not customarily acquire personal property for future leasing. But, under 12 CFR 23, they can do so, provided the acquisition is consistent with the following: the bank's current leasing business, a business plan for expansion of the bank's existing leasing business, or a business plan for entry into the leasing business. A bank may use this exception without having entered into a conforming lease, a legally binding agreement indemnifying the bank against loss in connection with the acquisition, or a legally binding commitment to lease. The bank's aggregate investment in property held pursuant to this exception can not exceed 15 percent of the bank's capital and surplus.

National banks should account for these assets consistent with generally accepted accounting principles (GAAP). So, assets acquired and held for future leasing activities should be recorded at cost. If the property is not leased or otherwise disposed of within a reasonable time frame, it should be reviewed for impairment.

Lending Limits

All leases entered into after June 12, 1979, are subject to the limits in 12 USC 84 and 12 CFR 32. The lease value used for the lending limits may not have any relation to the value recorded on the bank's books. The bank should record leases on its books according to SFAS 13. For lending limit purposes, the outstanding obligation of the lessee is calculated by summing the present value of both the lease payments and the residual value of the property.

The outstanding obligation of the lessee under a leveraged lease is calculated similarly. The examiner should deduct the unamortized balance of the non-recourse debt from the present value elements. The rate used in the present value equation is the "rate implicit in the lease" as SFAS 13 defines that term. In lieu of determining the present value, examiners may use the following formula as a quick estimate of the obligation of the lessee:

> Bank cost of acquisition of personal property minus the investment tax credit realized minus the balance of any nonrecourse debt.

If that value, which is equal to the one used initially to determine the lending limit, combined with the total of other obligations of the customer to the bank, is greater than the lending limit, examiners must determine the present value of the payments and residual value before citing a violation of the lending limit.

If a bank violates the lending limit with an advance of funds in the form of a lease, it may correct the violation by selling a participation that covers the amount by which the advance exceeds the legal lending limit at the time of its origination. The examiner should ensure that the bank does not sell an ownership interest in the leased property in such a way as to create a general partnership in which a bank, by law, may not participate.

General Procedures

Objective: To set the scope for assessing the quantity of risk and the quality of risk management in lease financing.

1. Review the following documents to identify any previously identified problems related to the leasing area that require follow-up:

   • Previous examination reports.
   • Follow-up activities.
   • Overall summary comments.
   • Work papers from previous examinations.
   • Internal and external audit reports.

   (Note: If an examiner is assigned Internal and external audit, a copy of any significant deficiencies for this area should be obtained from that examiner. If internal and external audit is not part of the overall scope of the examination, review the work performed by the internal and external auditors in this area and obtain a list of any deficiencies noted in their most recent review.)

2. Review the UBPR, BERT, and other applicable reports. Obtain any reports management uses to supervise the lease financing area. Examples include:

   • Trial balances.
   • Subsidiary controls.
   • General ledger.
   • Call report, if using a quarter-end examination date.
   • List of equity participations purchased and sold as of examination date, indicating from whom purchased or to whom sold.
   • List of past-due and defaulted leases, as of examination date, that gives the date of lease, terms, book value, residual value, date of last payment, description, and location of property.
   • Latest appraisal report or other collateral evaluation for past-due and defaulted leases.
   • Past-due and defaulted lease reports submitted to the board of directors or its loan or leasing committee.

- A schedule of lease commitments, as of examination date, that gives the name of the prospective lessee, the date of commitment, expiration date, cost, and description of property to be leased.
- A list of off-lease property, as of examination date, which discloses the book value, the date property came off lease, a description and location of property, the date of latest appraisal, and the appraised value.
- A list of liability and other information on common borrowers from examiners assigned cash items, overdrafts, and other loan areas.

3. Determine, during early discussion with management:

   - How management supervises the lease financing area.
   - Any significant changes in policies, practices, personnel, and control systems.
   - Any internal or external factors that could affect the lease financing area.

4. Based on the performance of the previous steps, combined with discussions with the EIC and other appropriate supervisors, determine the scope of this examination and set the examination objectives.

   Select from among the following examination procedures the steps that are necessary to meet those objectives. Seldom will an examination require every step to be performed.

5. As examination procedures are performed, test for compliance with established policies or practices and the existence of appropriate internal control processes. Identify any area with inadequate supervision and/or undue risk, and discuss with the EIC the need to perform additional procedures.

Quantity of Risk

Conclusion: The quantity of risk is (low, moderate, or high).

Objective: To evaluate the adequacy of credit quality, collateral, and collectibility as well as to determine the quantity of other risks in various types of lease financing activities.

For All Leases (Direct, Operating, and Leveraged)

1. Prepare for examination a sample of leases that in the examiner's judgment require in-depth review.

2. Using the list of liability and other information on common borrowers, decide who will review the borrowing relationship.

3. Using selected lessee liability records and document files, transcribe or download the following information onto line sheets:

   - Name of lessee.
   - Type of business and other affiliations.
   - Name(s) of guarantor(s).
   - Date lease was made.
   - Terms including options.
   - Expiration date of lease.
   - Date of last lease payment.
   - Aggregate unpaid rentals.
   - Description and location of property.
   - Cost of property.
   - Book value.
   - Residual value.
   - Accumulated depreciation.
   - Insurance coverage.
   - Corporate resolution to lease and/or guarantee.

   For leveraged leases transcribe or download the following additional information onto line sheets:

   - Bank's original investment.
   - Name of indenture trustee (person holding security interest in leased property for the benefit of the lenders).
   - Name(s) of lender(s).
   - Original amount financed by lender(s).

- Current amount owed lender(s).
- Terms of the debt.
- Maturity of the debt.
- Name of owner trustee (person holding title to the leased property for the benefit of the equity holders).
- Name of other equity participants and percentage of equity owned.

4. Request credit folders on all selected leases, and transcribe the following information to financial statement line sheets and comment line sheets.

- Balance sheet and profit and loss statements for the preceding three fiscal years.
- The most recent interim balance sheets and profit and loss statements.
- Projections of future operations, including cash flow debt servicing requirements, earnings, and lease commitments.
- Current financial information on any guarantors.
- Past and present borrowing records with the bank and outside credit inquiries.
- Relevant information from the loan officer's credit memorandums.

5. Check central liability file on lessee(s) selected for review who are suspected of having additional liability in other loan areas. Discuss any potential lending limit violations with the examiner assigned Loan Portfolio Management and the EIC.

6. Assess the reasonableness of the bank's calculation of the inherent gain or loss for each lease selected for review.

7. Analyze both current and projected yields computed by the bank for reasonableness and accuracy by:

- Comparing the yield against the bank's share of investment for leveraged leases.
- Tracing income and lease balances from the yield calculation to the general ledger.
- Obtaining a listing of unearned income-leasing account and reconciling the total to the general ledger liability account.

Go to the appropriate section on specific lease types for additional procedures (e.g., to evaluate credit quality).

Delinquent and Defaulted Leases

1. Evaluate the credit quality of each selected delinquent or defaulted lease by considering:

   • The lessee's ability to properly amortize the fixed obligations, including all present and proposed lease arrangements.

   • The correlation between projected and achieved operational results, with emphasis on cash flow.

   • Duration of adverse operating trends and prospects for the future.

   • The reasonableness of residual values and any exposure to income adjustments or loss on termination. Determine whether the residual value has been reviewed in the last 12 months.

   • The reasonableness of the latest appraisal report or other collateral evaluation.

   • The usefulness of the leased property to a third party given the condition of the property.

   • The status of any proposed sale or lease.

   • The support offered by other collateral

   • Potential exposure to income through the recapture of tax benefits or changes in tax laws or rates.

   • The support afforded by guarantors.

   • The support afforded by vendor support arrangements.

   • Accelerated payments in the early years of the lease.

   • Any concentration of leases.

2. Assign classification of credit and specific allowance allocation for each lease if appropriate.

3. Determine the cost to the bank of repossessing and selling the property or repossessing and converting it to income-producing status through re-lease.

4. Evaluate the reports submitted to the board of directors, or its loan or leasing committee, to evaluate if they are complete in their evaluation of risk factors, loss potential, and causes of delinquency or default, and if they propose a course of action.

Direct Financing and Operating Leases

1. Determine that the terms and conditions of selected direct financing and operating leases are appropriate.

2. Evaluate the credit quality of each selected direct finance or operating lease by considering:

   - The lessee's ability to properly amortize the fixed obligations, including all present and proposed lease arrangements.

   - The correlation between projected and achieved operational results, with emphasis on cash flow.

   - The reasonableness of residual values and any exposure to income adjustments or loss on termination. Determine whether the residual value has been reviewed in the last 12 months.

   - Potential exposure to income through the recapture of tax benefits or changes in tax laws or rates.

   - Possible adverse operating trends.

   - The support offered by other collateral.

   - The usefulness of the leased property to a third party, in the event of default.

   - The support afforded by guarantors.

   - The support afforded by vendor support arrangements.

   - The support offered by various payment structures such as accelerated payments in the early years of the lease.

   - Any concentration of leases.

3. Assign classification of credit and specific allowance allocation for each lease, if appropriate.

4. Based on the findings from the previous direct financing and operating lease procedures, determine whether additional sampling is needed to complete the following verification procedures. If so, select a sample of leases from the listing, and:

- Reconcile the trial balance of the lease liability records with subsidiary controls, the general ledger, and the call report if using a quarter-end examination date.

- Determine that the lease is properly categorized as an operating or direct financing lease.

- Prepare and mail confirmation forms to lessee. Confirmation forms should include a description and location of the property, monthly or annual rentals, terms, and other major provisions and options. The confirmation should also include the outstanding balance of lease receivables.

- Determine that (1) an order to purchase or a legally binding agreement indemnifying the bank against loss was executed before the bank was committed to purchase and deliver the property, or that (2) the acquisition of these assets is consistent with the bank's existing leasing business or with a business plan for expansion of the bank's existing leasing business or for entry into the leasing business.

- Determine that the files contain bills of sale, invoices, titles, or other evidence of ownership for the property leased.

- Ascertain that a properly executed noncancelable lease is held.

- Determine that the bank has recorded ground leases or waivers from owners or mortgage holders of property on which the leased property is located.

- Review insurance coverage and determine that property damage coverage is adequate relative to book value and that liability insurance is in effect.

- Determine that periodic inspection reports are being received.

- When a lease is to a corporation, determine that corporate resolutions to lease have been executed.

5. For operating leases selected above:

- Reconcile the bank's recorded cost of the property to purchase invoices and payment drafts.
- Compare rental income from operating leases in the general ledger to the amounts of stated rents in the individual leases.
- Check the computation of any investment tax credit. (This credit was repealed effective January 1, 1986, but is mentioned in case a credit is reintroduced.)

6. For direct financing leases selected above:

- Verify that the lease receivable amount is correctly recorded and includes minimum rental payments plus residual value.
- Compare the amount of the lease payments to the lease agreement.
- Recalculate the amount of unearned income.
- Ensure that the proper lease amounts are recorded in the general ledger.

Leveraged Leases

1. Determine that terms and conditions of selected leveraged leases are appropriate.

2. Evaluate the credit quality of each selected leveraged lease by considering:

- The lessee's ability to properly amortize the fixed obligations, including all present and proposed lease arrangements.

- The correlation between projected and achieved operational results, with emphasis on cash flow.

- The reasonableness of residual values and any exposure to income adjustments or loss on termination. Determine whether the residual value has been reviewed in the last 12 months.

- Potential exposure to income through the recapture of tax benefits or changes in tax laws or rates.

- Possible adverse operating trends.

- The support offered by other collateral.

- The usefulness of the leased property to a third party, in the event of default.

- The support afforded by guarantors.

- The support afforded by vendor support arrangements.

- The support offered by various payment structures such as accelerated payments in the early years of the lease.

- Any concentration of leases.

4. Assign classification of credit and specific allowance allocation for each lease if appropriate.

5. Determine that provisions in the lease for default, early termination because of obsolescence, and casualty loss agree with the terms of debt.

6. Determine that the lease and debt permit equity holder(s) to correct or prevent defaults and foreclosures by fulfilling the obligations of the lessee or repaying the debt early.

7. Determine that all debt instruments contain a nonrecourse provision that negates any bank liability.

8. Determine whether the bank has obtained a favorable Internal Revenue Service ruling on the tax benefits and whether the lessee has indemnified the lessor against the loss of tax benefits because of future changes in tax laws.

9. Based on findings of previous leveraged lease procedures, determine whether additional sampling is needed to complete the following verification procedures. If so, using appropriate sampling techniques, select a sample of leases from the listing, and:

- Reconcile the trial balance of leveraged lease records to subsidiary controls, the general ledger, and the call report if using a quarter-end examination date.

- Determine that the lease is properly categorized as a leveraged lease.

- Prepare and mail confirmation forms to lessee. Confirmation forms should include a description and location of the property, monthly or annual rentals, terms, outstanding balance, and other major provisions and options.

- Determine that (1) an order to purchase or a legally binding agreement indemnifying the bank against loss was executed before the bank was committed to purchase and deliver the property, or that (2) the acquisition of these assets is consistent with the bank's existing leasing business or with a business plan for expansion of the bank's existing leasing business or for entry into the leasing business.
- Determine that the files contain bills of sale, invoices, titles, or other evidence of ownership for the property leased.
- Ascertain that a properly executed noncancelable lease is held.
- Determine that the bank has recorded ground leases or waivers from owners or mortgage holders of property on which the leased property is located.
- Review insurance coverage and determine that property damage coverage is adequate relative to book value and that liability insurance is in effect.
- Determine that periodic inspection reports are being received.
- When a lease is to a corporation, determine that corporate resolutions to lease have been executed.
- Check monthly payments to loan participants to ensure interest expense is properly recorded.
- Verify that the investment is recorded in accordance with SFAS 13.
- Verify that the lease income is recognized properly in accordance with SFAS 13.
- Review assumptions (tax position, residual value, etc.) the bank uses in its analysis for reasonableness.
- Check the computation of any investment tax credit. (This credit was repealed effective January 1, 1986, but is mentioned in case a credit is reintroduced.)
- If the bank is a lender, follow appropriate verification procedures for the type of loan involved.

For Leveraged Leases — Equity Participations

In addition to the procedures detailed above for leveraged leases, perform the following steps for equity participations:

1. Determine that all participations are without recourse.

2. Determine that the bank has taken the necessary steps to ensure that it does not become a general partner with the participants.

3. Compare participations purchased to approvals recorded in minutes of board of directors or committee meetings.

Commitments to Lease

1. Using the schedule of lease commitments, select items for examination.

2. Evaluate the ability of selected prospective lessees to service the anticipated obligation.

3. Evaluate reasonableness of estimated residual value.

4. Compare lease commitments to approvals recorded in minutes of board of directors or committee meetings.

Off-Lease Property

1. Determine the reason for off-lease status.

2. Evaluate the reasonableness of the latest appraisal or other collateral evaluation and evaluate condition of the property.

3. Determine the cost to the bank of selling the property or converting it to income-producing status through re-lease.

4. Determine the status of any proposed sale or lease.

5. Assign classification of credit and specific allowance allocation for each off-lease property if appropriate.

6. Determine whether the bank disposes of off-lease property as soon as practical.

7. Determine whether any of the property has been off-lease for five years or more. If so, determine whether the bank received an extension from the OCC.

8. Balance the aggregate book value to general ledger.

Property Acquired for Future Leasing Activity

1. Obtain a list, as of examination date, of all property acquired and held for future leasing activities. The list should include the date the property was acquired, the book value of the property, and the original cost of the property.

2. Determine that the acquisition of these assets is consistent with the bank's existing leasing business or consistent with a business plan for expansion

of the bank's existing leasing business or for entry into the leasing business as required by 12 CFR 23.4(b)(1).

- Obtain all subsidiary asset ledgers, foot on a test basis, and check against the general ledger control accounts.
- Test the propriety of significant acquisitions. To do so, compare each such acquisition's cost with that of similar assets, review the method used to select a vendor, and inspect the asset in person.
- Test the propriety of the lease price by comparing the price with that of similar assets and by reviewing the method used to establish the lease price.

3. Determine whether property held for an extended period has been reviewed for impairment of value. If the value of property is permanently impaired, ensure that the bank has written down the book value to reflect the impairment.

Compliance with Laws, Rules, and Regulations

Objective: To determine compliance with applicable laws, rulings, and regulations for various types of lease financing activities.

For All Leases (12 CFR 23 Subpart A)

1. Determine that rentals, estimated tax benefits, and the estimated residual value of the property at the expiration of the term are such that the bank can reasonably expect to realize the return of its full investment in the leased property plus the estimated cost of financing the property over the term of the lease.

2. Determine that all leases are net leases under which the bank is not directly or indirectly responsible for servicing, repair, maintenance, purchasing of parts and accessories, or insuring the leased property.

3. Determine that any purchase of property is consistent with the provisions of 12 CFR 23.4(a) or (b).

4. Determine whether the bank specifically identifies any records it maintains on its CEBA leases in a manner that distinguishes them from records on 12 USC 24 (Seventh) leases.

5. Determine whether financing arrangements meet the limits on loans or extensions of credit under 12 USC 84.

6. Determine whether financing arrangements meet the restrictions on transactions with affiliates under 12 USC 371c and 371c-1.

For CEBA Leases (12 CFR 23 Subpart B)

1. Determine that the aggregate book value of all tangible personal property held under CEBA leases does not exceed 10 percent of consolidated bank assets.

2. Determine that the initial lease term was not less than 90 days.

For 12 USC 24 (Seventh) Leases (12 CFR 23 Subpart C)

1. Determine that the estimate of the unguaranteed portion of the residual value is reasonable and does not exceed 25 percent of the original cost.

2. Determine that all leases represent noncancelable obligations of the lessee.

For Leases of Real Property to a Municipality or Public Authority (12 CFR 7.1000(d))

1. Determine that the lessee has resources sufficient to make payments on all rentals as they become due. Sufficient resources may be demonstrated by general taxing ability.

2. Determine that the lease agreement provides that, upon expiration, the lessee becomes title holder of the property.

For Property Acquired for Future Leasing Activities

1. Determine that the bank's aggregate investment in property acquired for future leasing activities does not exceed 15 percent of the bank's capital and surplus as specified in 12 CFR 23.4(b)(2).

Quality of Risk Management

Conclusion: The quality of risk management is (weak, acceptable, or strong).

Policy

Conclusion: The board (has/has not) established effective policies regarding lease financing.

Objective: To determine whether lease policies are adequate and whether the board of directors has adopted effective lease policies and practices.

1. Review the bank's lease financing policies and practices. Do they:

   - Establish procedures for reviewing lease financing applications?
   - Define types of leasing activities that the bank will consider, including any limits?
   - Define qualified property?
   - Establish minimum standards for documentation?

2. Determine whether lease financing policies and practices are reviewed at least annually by the board of directors. Does the board of directors determine whether policies are compatible with changing market conditions?

Processes

Conclusion: Management and the board (have/have not) established effective processes regarding lease financing.

Objective: Determine the adequacy of lease administration processes.

1. Determine the quality of reports available to effectively administer lease financing. Consider the following:

   - Are periodic property inventory reports prepared by the lessee or trustee?
   - Do reports clearly indicate the condition and location of property?

- Does the board of directors, at its regular meetings, receive for review reports listing leases that are past due, criticized, or receiving special attention?
- Does the board of directors receive accurate reports on lease transaction yields?

2. Assess the bank's process for obtaining inspections on leased personal property. If inspection of the leased property is either infrequent or not feasible, has the bank taken measures to protect its personal property and prevent its misuse?

3. Review the bank's procedures for accepting bids for the purchase of the leased property at termination of the lease to ensure that reasonable estimates of value are obtained. For a lease with no specific purchase options or renewal or extension periods, does the bank require outside appraisals or other reasonable estimates of value before accepting a bid for the purchase of the leased property?

4. Determine whether review procedures are in effect to maintain the necessary insurance coverage on all leased assets. Does the bank's insurance coverage include its potential public liability risk as owner-lessor of the property?

5. Review the adequacy of safeguards in effect to prevent the possibility of a conflict of interest or self-dealing in selecting the following:

- Seller of the leased property.
- Servicer of the leased property.
- Insurer of the leased property.
- Purchaser of the leased property.

6. Review the approval process for leases to determine whether:

- Provisions within the normal credit policy are met.
- The originating loan officer(s) or loan/lease committee have adequate lending authority.
- Modifications of terms require the approval of the board or the lease committee that initially approved the lease.

7. Review the process to ensure that leases are supported by current credit information.

8. Determine whether commitments are contingent upon receipt of certain satisfactory information. If so, is someone other than the account officer responsible for rejecting or accepting that information?

9. Determine whether the bank's manner of establishing and updating residual values on leased property is in accordance with generally accepted accounting principles. Consider whether:

- Residual values are reviewed annually.
- Residual write-downs are in accordance with SFAS 13, if there is a permanent decline in value.
- The bank uses modeling to derive residual values, whether or not assumptions are reasonable.
- Residual schedules balance.

10. Determine whether the bank's manner of establishing the depreciable life of leased property and depreciation methods are reasonable and in accordance with generally accepted accounting principles. The examiner should consider:

- Testing the footings of the depreciation schedules.
- Tracing depreciation expense from depreciation schedules to the subsidiary and general ledgers.

11. Review the bank's practice of accounting for terminated leases by reviewing leases terminated since the previous examination. Consider whether:

- Terminated leases are properly recorded.
- The sales price for personal property that has been sold was reasonable.
- Any gain or loss on the termination is calculated accurately.

Personnel

Conclusion: The board, management, and affected personnel (do/do not) possess the skills and knowledge required to manage and perform duties related to lease financing.

Objective: Given the size and complexity of the bank, determine whether bank management/personnel possess and display acceptable knowledge and technical skills in managing and performing duties related to lease financing.

1. Determine significant current and previous work experience of management and leasing personnel. Consider:

- Specialized lending experience (i.e., leveraged leasing).
- Tax and accounting experience.

2. Determine whether management and leasing personnel are well-educated in lease financing and whether they plan further education in the subject.
3. Assess technical knowledge and ability to manage leasing operations using results of lease administration evaluation and determination of the quantity of risk.

Controls

Conclusion: Management (has/has not) established effective control systems.

Objective: To determine the effectiveness of control systems employed to manage lease financing.

1. Determine the effectiveness of the loan review system in identifying risk in lease financing. Consider the following:

   - Scope of review.
   - Frequency of reviews.
   - Qualifications of loan review personnel.
   - Examination results.

2. Determine the adequacy of the audit function for lease finance activities. Consider the following:
   - Scope of the internal audit.
   - Frequency of reviews.
   - Qualifications of internal audit personnel.

3. Determine whether management has appropriately addressed concerns and areas of unwarranted risk.

4. Determine whether management information systems are capable of accurately gathering and tracking information and providing needed reports.

5. Determine whether the appropriate operational tools exist to safeguard assets and ensure the integrity of accounting data/financial reports for lease financing. Consider the following:

   For Lease Financing Records

   - Are separate files maintained for each lease transaction?
   - Does each file supporting the acquisition and disposal of assets reflect the review and written approval of an officer other than the person who controlled the disbursement and receipt of funds?

- Is the preparation and posting of subsidiary lease financing records performed or reviewed by persons who do not also:
  - Issue official checks and drafts singly?
  - Handle cash?
- Are the subsidiary lease financing records reconciled to the appropriate general ledger accounts at least monthly, and are reconciling items investigated by persons who do not also handle cash?
- Are delinquent account collection requests and past-due notices checked to the trial balances, and are they handled only by persons who do not also handle cash?
- Are inquiries about lease balances received and investigated by persons who do not also handle cash?
- Are documents supporting recorded credit adjustments checked or tested subsequently by persons who do not also handle cash?
- Does the bank maintain records adequate to determine whether total CEBA leases exceed 10 percent of consolidated bank assets?

For Interest and Rent

- Is the preparation and posting of interest and rent records performed or reviewed by persons who do not also:
  - Issue official checks and drafts singly?
  - Handle cash?

For Depreciation (Operating and Leveraged Leases)

- Is the preparation and posting of periodic depreciation records performed or reviewed by persons who do not also have sole custody of property?
- Do the bank's procedures require that depreciation expense be charged at least quarterly?
- Are the subsidiary depreciation records balanced to the appropriate general ledger controls at least quarterly by persons who do not also have sole custody of property?

For Property Acquired for Future Leasing Activity

- Do the bank's procedures preclude persons who have access to property from having "sole custody of property" in that:
  - Its physical character or use would make any unauthorized use or disposal readily apparent?
  - Inventory control methods sufficiently limit accessibility?
- Is the addition, lease, or other disposal of property approved by the signature of an officer who does not also control the related disbursement or receipt of funds?

- Is the preparation and maintenance of property subsidiary records for additions, leases, and other disposals performed or reviewed by persons who do not have sole custody of the property?
- Are subsidiary property records balanced, at least quarterly, to the appropriate general ledger accounts by persons who do not also have sole custody of property?
- Is the existence of property checked or tested, such as in a physical inventory, and are any differences between the property's characteristics and its description in property records investigated by persons who do not also have sole custody of equipment?
- Does the bank maintain separate property files that include bills of sale, invoices, titles, or other evidence of ownership?

Conclusion Procedures

Objective: To communicate findings and initiate corrective action when policies, practices, procedures, objectives, or internal controls are deficient or when violations of law, rulings, or regulations have been noted.

1. Provide EIC with brief conclusion regarding:

   - The adequacy of the bank's policies or practices regarding leases.
   - How bank officers conform to established policy or practices.
   - Adverse trends in the leasing department.
   - Internal control deficiencies or exceptions.
   - Any corrective action recommended for deficient policies, practices, or procedures.
   - The quality of departmental management.
   - The quantity of credit/residual risk in the portfolio.
   - The adequacy of MIS.
   - Other matters of significance.

2. Determine the impact on the aggregate and direction of risk assessments for any applicable risks identified while performing the foregoing procedures. Examiners should refer to guidance provided under the OCC's large and community bank risk assessment programs.

   - Risk Categories: Compliance, Credit, Foreign Exchange, Interest Rate, Liquidity, Price, Reputation, Strategic, Transaction
   - Risk Conclusions: High, Moderate, or Low
   - Risk Direction: Increasing, Stable, or Declining

3. Determine, in consultation with EIC, whether the risks identified are significant enough to merit bringing them to the board's attention in the report of examination. If so, prepare items for inclusion in "Matters Requiring Board Attention" (MRBA).

   - MRBA should cover practices that :
     - Deviate from sound fundamental principles and are likely to result in financial deterioration if not addressed.
     - Result in substantive noncompliance with laws.
   - MRBA should discuss:
     - Causes of the problem.
     - Consequences of inaction.
     - Management's commitment to corrective action.
     - The time frame and person(s) responsible for corrective action.

4. Discuss findings with management including conclusions regarding applicable risks. Include the following subjects, if relevant:

- Delinquent leases.
- Violations of laws, rulings, and regulations.
- Leases not supported by current and complete financial information.
- Leases for which documentation is deficient.
- Personal property deficiencies revealed in inspection reports.
- Off-lease personal property.
- Concentrations of leases.
- Classified leases.
- Leases to major shareholders, employees, officers, directors, or the interests of officers or directors.

5. As appropriate, prepare a brief comment on lease financing for the report of examination. In general terms, address the following subjects:

- Quantity of risk.
- Quality of risk management.

6. Prepare a memorandum or update the work program with any information that will facilitate future examinations.

7. Update the ongoing supervisory record and any applicable report of examination schedules or tables.

8. Organize and reference working papers in accordance with OCC guidance.

Example 1

The following is a description of an operating lease on office equipment:

Lessor's cost of the leased property	$10,000
Fair value of the leased property at inception of the lease . .	$10,000
Monthly lease payments	$ 270
Residual value (not guaranteed) at end of lease	$ 4,000
Present value of lease payments discounted at the implicit interest rate of 12.04 percent	$ 7,035
Economic life of the property	60 months
Lease term	30 months

The lease does not transfer ownership of the property to the lessee at the end of the lease, nor does it contain a bargain purchase agreement. Further, collection of the minimum lease payments is reasonably predictable, as is the amount of unreimbursed costs to be incurred by the lessor.

With respect to the capitalization criteria:

- The lease does not transfer ownership of the property at the end of the lease.
- The lease does not contain a bargain purchase option.
- The lease term is less than 75 percent of the estimated economic life of the equipment.
- The present value ($7,035) of the minimum lease payments is less than 90 percent of the fair value of the property.

Accordingly, since the lease does not meet any of the capitalization criteria set forth in "Accounting for Leases" in this booklet, it would be classified as an operating lease.

The journal entry on the books of the lessor to record this operating lease is as follows:

Office equipment	$10,000	
Cash		$10,000
To record the purchase of the office equipment.		

The following entries are recorded monthly:

```
Cash  ............................    $   270
    Rental income  ......................              $   270
        To record the monthly rental income.

Depreciation expense  .................    $   200
    Accumulated depreciation ............              $   200
        To record the monthly depreciation.
```

Example 2

The following is a description of a capital lease on office equipment:

Lessor's cost of the leased property	$10,000
Fair value of the leased property at inception of the lease ..	$10,000
Monthly lease payments	$ 245
Residual value (not guaranteed) at end of lease	$ 1,000
Present value of lease payments discounted at the implicit interest rate of 12.09 percent	$ 9,382
Economic life of the property	60 months
Lease term	48 months

The lease does not transfer ownership of the property to the lessee at the end of the lease, nor does it contain a bargain purchase agreement. Further, collection of the minimum lease payments is reasonably predictable as is the amount of unreimbursed costs to be incurred by the lessor.

With respect to the capitalization criteria:

- The lease does not transfer ownership of the property at the end of the lease.
- The lease does not contain a bargain purchase option.
- The lease term is more than 75 percent of the estimated economic life of the equipment.
- The present value ($9,382) of the minimum lease payments is more than 90 percent of the fair value of the property.

Since the lease meets at least one of the capitalization criteria and both of the qualifications in "Accounting for Leases," it must be classified as a direct financing (i.e., capital) lease. (In this example, the lease met two of the criteria. However, meeting any of the criteria would cause it to be classified as a capital lease, provided the two qualifications are met.

The journal entries on the books of the lessor to record this direct financing lease are as follows:

Office equipment	$10,000	
Cash		$10,000
To record the purchase of the office equipment.		

Lease receivable, gross	$12,760	
Office equipment		$ 10,000
Unearned income		$ 2,760
To record the lease as a direct financing lease.		

The following entries are recorded monthly:

Cash	$ 245	
Lease receivable		$ 245
To record the lease payment.		

Unearned income	$ 98	
Interest income		$ 98
To record the interest income earned during the month. (This entry will be recorded monthly. However, the amount will decrease as the outstanding balance of the lease receivable decreases.)		

Example 3

The following is a description of a leveraged lease on equipment:

Lessor's cost of the leased property	$500,000
Residual value (not guaranteed) at end of lease	$ 50,000
Annual lease payments	$ 86,250
Lease term	8 years
Depreciable life of property for tax purposes	5 years

Financing:

Equity investment by lessor	$100,000
Long-term nonrecourse debt at 10 percent	$400,000

Depreciation allowable to lessor for income tax purposes .. $500,000

Lessor's income tax rate (federal and state) 40%

The following is a schedule of the lessor's debt amortization.[1]

Year	Cash Payment	Interest Exp. @ 10%	Principal Reduction	Unamortized Principal
Initial Balance				400,000
1	74,978	40,000	34,978	365,022
2	74,978	36,502	38,476	326,546
3	74,978	32,655	42,323	284,223
4	74,978	28,422	46,556	237,667
5	74,978	23,767	51,211	186,456
6	74,978	18,646	56,332	130,123
7	74,978	13,012	61,966	68,158
8	74,978	6,820	68,158	(0)
	599,824	199,824	400,000	

---

1   For simplicity, this table assumes one annual payment at the end of each year. In practice, lease payments are generally made at the beginning of each month.

Unlike income on nonleveraged leases, income on leveraged leases is allocated as after-tax cash flow. The after-tax cash flow must be calculated for each accounting period. In order to make this calculation, the annual taxable income and resultant tax liability is computed. These amounts are presented in the following table.

Year	Rental Income	Depr. Expense[2]	Interest Expense	Taxable Income\Loss	Tax Savings (Expense)[3]
1	86,250	150,000	40,000	(103,750)	41,500
2	86,250	120,000	36,502	(70,252)	28,101
3	86,250	90,000	32,655	(36,405)	14,562
4	86,250	60,000	28,422	(2,172)	869
5	86,250	30,000	23,767	32,483	(12,993)
6	86,250	0	18,646	67,604	(27,042)
7	86,250	0	13,012	73,238	(29,295)
8	136,250[4]	50,000[5]	6,820	79,430	(31,772)
	740,000	500,000	199,824	40,176	(16,070)

---

2   For federal income tax purposes.

3   At an assumed federal/state combined tax rate of 40 percent.

4   Includes the proceeds from the sale of the residual value.

5   Represents remaining cost related to residual value.

Once the annual income-tax effect has been computed, the after-tax cash flow can be calculated:

Year	Rental Income	Interest Expense	Principal Reduction	Tax Savings (Expense)	Annual Cash Flow[6]
Initial Investment					(100,000)
1	86,250	40,000	34,978	41,500	52,772
2	86,250	36,502	38,476	28,101	39,373
3	86,250	32,655	42,323	14,562	25,834
4	86,250	28,422	46,556	869	12,141
5	86,250	23,767	51,211	(12,993)	(1,721)
6	86,250	18,646	56,332	(27,042)	(15,770)
7	86,250	13,012	61,966	(29,295)	(18,023)
8	136,250	6,820	68,158	(31,772)	29,500
	740,000	199,824	400,000	(16,070)	24,106

6   Rental income plus tax savings (or less tax expense) less interest expense and principal reduction.

Based on the original investment and the expected after-tax cash flows, a constant rate of return is computed for each year in which there is a positive investment. Income is allocated based on this constant rate.

| Year | Investment in Lease Beginning of Year | Annual Cash Flows[7] | | | Investment in Lease End of Year |
		Total	Allocate to Income (after tax)	Allocate to Investment	
1	100,000	52,772	10,966	41,806	58,194
2	58,194	39,373	6,381	32,992	25,202
3	25,202	25,834	2,764	23,070	2,132
4	2,132	12,141	234	11,907	(9,775)
5	(9,775)	(1,721)	0	(1,721)	(8,054)
6	(8,054)	(15,770)	0	(15,770)	7,716
7	7,716	(18,023)	846	(18,869)	26,585
8	26,585	29,500	2,915	26,585	0
		124,106	24,106	100,000	

---

7   Lease income is recognized as 10.97percent of the unrecovered investment at the beginning of each year in which the net investment is positive. This rate, when applied to the net investment of years that have a positive balance at the beginning of the year, determines the after-tax net income in those years.

Even though the yield on a leveraged lease is computed on an after-tax basis, the lease is recorded and accounted for on a pre-tax basis. Accordingly, the following journal entries record the acquisition of the property and the lease activity during the first year of the lease:

At origination:

Lease receivable	$140,176	
Unearned income		$ 40,176
Cash		$100,000

    To record the initial investment in the lease. Unearned income is the sum of the annual pre-tax cash flows.

At end of year one:

Cash	$ 11,272	
Lease receivable		$ 11,272

    Collection of first year's rent net of mortgage payments. Represents annual rental payments less debt payments.

Unearned income	$ 18,276	
Rental income		$ 18,276

    Recognition of first year's portion of pre-tax unearned income allocated in the same proportion as after-tax income allocation on page 44.

Income tax payable (receivable)	$ 41,500	
Income tax expense	$ 7,310	
Deferred income tax liability		$ 48,810

    To record the first year's tax credit from operations and to recognize deferred taxes.

Bargain purchase option. A provision allowing the lessee the option of purchasing the leased property for an amount lower than the expected fair value of the property at the date the option becomes exercisable.

Bargain renewal option. A provision allowing the lessee the option of renewing the lease for an amount lower than the expected rental for equivalent property under similar terms and conditions at the date the option becomes exercisable.

CEBA leases. Lease activities allowed under section 108 of the Competitive Equality Banking Act of 1987 and permissible under 12 USC 24 (10th).

Estimated economic life of the leased property. The period over which one or more users can expect the property to be economical when used for its intended purpose.

Fair value of leased property. The property's selling price in an arm's-length transaction between unrelated parties.

Full–payout lease. A lease in which the national bank reasonably expects to realize the return of its full investment in the leased property, plus the estimated cost of financing the property over the term of the lease, from rentals, estimated tax benefits, and the estimated residual value of the property.

Gross investment in leases. The sum of the minimum lease payments (including any guarantee of residual value), unguaranteed estimated residual value of the property, and investment tax credit, if applicable.

Implicit interest rate. The discount rate (interest rate) that would make the aggregate present value of the minimum lease payment and the unguaranteed residual equal the fair value of the property at the inception of the lease less any investment tax credit retained by the lessor.

Incremental borrowing rate. The interest rate the lessee would have had to pay, at inception of the lease, to borrow funds to purchase the leased asset.

Indenture trustee. An individual chosen to hold the mortgage on leased property on behalf of debt participants. Such trustees are most common in leveraged leases involving many parties.

Initial direct costs. Costs that are directly associated with the origination of the leasing transaction. They are incurred by the lessor and paid to independent third parties.

Lease term. The fixed, noncancelable term of the lease plus the following: bargain renewal options, ordinary renewal options before the bargain renewal option is exercisable, renewals, extensions at the lessor's option, and any period during which failure to renew penalizes the lessee sufficiently to make renewal appear reasonably certain.

Minimum lease payments. The sum of the payments over the noncancelable term of the lease plus any residual payments guaranteed by the lessee or a creditworthy unrelated third party.

Net investment in a lease. The gross investment less any unamortized unearned income arising from the transaction.

Net lease. A lease under which the national bank-lessor will not, directly or indirectly, provide or be obligated to provide for:

(1)   Servicing, repair, or maintenance of the leased property during the lease term;

(2)   Parts or accessories for the leased property;

(3)   Loan of replacement or substitute property while the leased property is being serviced;

(4)   Payment of insurance for the lessee, except when the lessee has failed in its contractual obligation to purchase or maintain required insurance; or

(5)   Renewal of any license or registration for the property unless renewal by the lessor is necessary to protect its interest as owner or financier of the property.

Noncancelable lease. A lease that cannot be canceled without the permission of the lessor or unless circumstances develop that appear to be remote possibilities at the inception of the lease.

Nonrecourse debt. Borrowed funds that give the creditor recourse only to the specific property being financed. The creditor has no right to the borrower's other assets.

Off-lease property.   Property that was subject to a lease that has been terminated and that is now being held by the bank before being sold, re-leased, or otherwise disposed of.

Owner trustee.   An individual chosen to hold title to leased property on behalf of equity participants. Such a trustee is most common in leveraged leases involving many parties.

Residual value of leased property.   The estimated fair value of leased property at the end of the noncancelable lease term.

Unguaranteed residual value. The estimated residual value at the end of the lease term less any portion guaranteed by the lessee or any third party unrelated to the lessor.

Unearned income. The total income expected to be earned over the remaining life of the lease. At inception, unearned income is the difference between the lessor's investment in the property and the gross investment in the lease. Unearned income has three components: minimum lease payments, unguaranteed residual value, and investment tax credit.

General Power

Laws

12 USC 24 (Seventh), Corporate powers of associations
12 USC 24 (10th), Corporate powers of associations
12 USC 84, Lending limits

Regulations

12 CFR 23, Leasing
12 CFR 32, Lending limits

Power for Leasing Public Facilities

Regulations

12 CFR 7.1000(d), National bank ownership of property

Accounting

SFAS 13, Statement of Financial Accounting Standards No. 13, "Accounting for Leases"

OCC Bank Accounting Advisory Series, BAAS, Topic 5 — "Leases"